To:

From:

D0536955

10 Ways to Use
WALK *the* TALK

1. A training and **development tool**.

2. A **meeting or convention gift** to reinforce your theme.

3. A resource to **motivate and inspire your team**.

4. A thank you for **"going the extra mile."**

5. A gift to celebrate a **company milestone**.

6. A year-end **"thanks for your business"** gift.

7. A tool to encourage **"best in class"** customer service.

8. A **"first order"** thank you gift.

9. A **"leave behind"** or "thank you" gift for salespeople to use.

10. A gift to your best prospects saying, **"We're still here, we still care, and here's what you can expect from us."**

WALK *the* TALK

Eric Harvey   Steve Ventura

Co-published by:

WALKTHETALK.COM™
1100 Parker Square, Suite 250
Flower Mound, TX 75028
888.822.9255

SIMPLE TRUTHS®
1952 McDowell Road, Suite 205
Naperville, IL 60563
800.900.3427

PHOTO CREDITS:
Page 39: © 2007 Corbis/Jupiterimages
Pages 58-59: © 2007 Dan Nourie /Glasshouse Images/Jupiterimages
Page 67: © 2007 Leighty, Bruce/Index Stock Imagery/Jupiterimages
Pages 82-83: © 2007 Jupiterimages Corporation
All other images © 2007 iStockphoto.com

Designed by Vieceli Design Company
Edited by Michelle Sedas

Printed and bound in the United States of America.
www.WalkTheTalk.com   www.simpletruths.com
02   WOZ   08

TABLE OF CONTENTS

Integrity
Trust
Responsibility

With few exceptions, all of us have beliefs, values, and a relatively similar sense of what's right and what's wrong. They are what make us different from other living things on the planet ... they are what make us human.

But while having principles may be natural for us, actually practicing them isn't. Acting according to these beliefs, values, and good intentions ... doing what's right ... **"walking the talk"** is one of the biggest challenges each of us faces every day. It's true for just about every aspect of our lives – from family and faith, to sports and politics, to our jobs and our communities.

Honesty

Commitment

Respect

Unquestionably, talking about (or in our case, writing about) beliefs is easy — there's not much effort or pain involved at all. **Behaving** those values, however, is quite another story.

Discussing good citizenship is a lot easier than going out in an election-day rainstorm to vote. Stating the importance of honesty is just plain easier than overcoming the temptation to keep the change the store clerk overpays us. Touting good service is one thing, staying late to make sure a customer is taken care of is quite another. And, waxing eloquent about how parents should be actively involved in their children's education is a piece of cake compared to turning off our most favorite TV program so we can check our children's homework.

The list is endless and timeless, and the basis of some very familiar phrases:

PRACTICE WHAT YOU PREACH

ACTIONS SPEAK LOUDER THAN WORDS

TALK IS CHEAP

SHOW ME

and the song title

A LITTLE LESS TALK AND A LOT MORE ACTION.

Here are two facts "you can take to the bank":

 1. We all have moments when our behaviors are out of sync with the beliefs we hold deep down inside, and

2. The vast majority of those out-of-sync behaviors are UNintentional.

Think about it. How many times have you jumped out of bed in the morning and declared, "My mission in life today is to NOT walk my talk. I'm not gonna rest until I'm out of sync somehow, some way!"? We'll go way out on a limb and guess that your answer is NEVER! It just doesn't happen that way.

Are there some misguided, hypocritical people out there who knowingly — even intentionally — do wrong? Unfortunately, yes. They're the ones who make the headlines. The good news, however, is that they're also the extreme exceptions. The rest of us tend to approach each new day loaded with noble goals and good intentions.

But too often, we get bombarded with demands, crises, pressures, changes, issues, and unexpected situations that make merely "holding our own" sometimes the best that we can hope for. As a result, it can become way too easy to fly through our lives on automatic pilot — without really thinking about what we do and whether or not we're actually **behaving** our beliefs.

To be sure, living according to our "guiding principles" – and those of the organizations for which we work – takes conscious effort, persistence, some courage, a good-size helping of commitment, and a ton of self-discipline.

IF IT WAS EASY, WE WOULDN'T NEED THOSE ATTRIBUTES IN ORDER TO SUCCEED.

IF IT WAS EASY, IT WOULDN'T BE A "CHALLENGE."

IF IT WAS EASY, EVERYBODY WOULD DO IT ALL THE TIME.

Walking the talk is no different than any other aspect of life. We all have moments of sheer brilliance and achievement. We set goals for ourselves, zero in on the target, and hit the bull's-eye smack-dab in the center.

But, there are also times when our aim is a little off or when we miss the target altogether.

WHO AMONG US CAN'T IMPROVE A LITTLE (OR A LOT) AS A PARENT, SPOUSE, FRIEND, PARTNER, CITIZEN, EMPLOYEE, OR LEADER?

Since no one is perfect, common sense suggests that no one can ever walk the talk perfectly, all the time. The absence of perfection leaves more than enough room for improvement for all of us.

When it comes to bringing values to life – to doing the good, right, and appropriate thing ...

**We're always working at it.
We're never totally there.
And the challenge starts
all over again with
each new tomorrow.**

FIVE
KEY PRINCIPLES

Some time, in the not-too-distant future, these will probably be known as "the good old days." But for now, they're just the times in which we live. And they are challenging times, indeed. More and more we find ourselves facing situations which test our human fiber ... and our moral compass. **Temptations to do what's convenient, easy, and self-serving come at us like waves rushing to the shore.**

How do we deal with this reality? How can we ensure that we stay on the right path and avoid compromising our values and beliefs? **We do it by continually reflecting on the following five key principles of walking the talk ... and acting accordingly.**

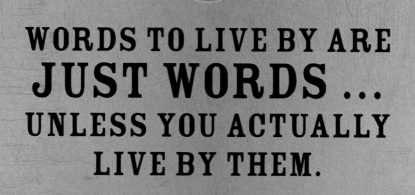

1

WORDS TO LIVE BY ARE JUST WORDS ... UNLESS YOU ACTUALLY LIVE BY THEM.

we could change the world tomorrow if all
the millions of people around the world
acted the way they believe."

~ JANE GOODALL ~

FIVE KEY PRINCIPLES

YOU ARE
WHAT YOU DO.

Men **ACQUIRE** a particular quality by constantly
acting in a particular way.
We **BECOME** just by **PERFORMING**
just actions, temperate by
performing temperate actions,
brave by performing brave actions.

~ ARISTOTLE ~

EVERYTHING
YOU DO COUNTS.

THERE IS NEVER A WRONG TIME TO
DO THE RIGHT THING.

In the game of life, there are no time-outs. Unlike children at play, we don't get to call for do-overs – we don't get to cross our fingers, call a "mulligan," and claim that something we did doesn't count. Fact is, as adults, **all** of our actions matter ... **everything** we do counts! And that's especially true when it comes to living according to our beliefs and values.

Think about it. If it's wrong to take what isn't ours, then when is it okay to keep the extra change that a store clerk mistakenly overpays us? If it's wrong to lie, then when is it okay to "fudge" on an expense report or time sheet? If it's wrong to disrespect others, then when is it okay to tell racially oriented jokes? The answer to all three of those questions is the same:

IT'S NEVER OKAY!

To believe otherwise is to assume that the importance of doing what's right varies with the circumstances at hand. That's a slippery slope that we all need to avoid.

INTEGRITY IS NOT A
NINETY PERCENT THING ...
NOT A NINETY-FIVE PERCENT THING.
EITHER YOU HAVE IT,
OR YOU DON'T.

~ PETER SCOTESE ~

THE "GOLDEN RULE"
IS STILL
PURE GOLD.

It's an "old saying" – uttered seemingly forever – that is as familiar to us as the air that we breathe. It's a fundamental moral principle found in virtually all major religions and cultures around the world. Everywhere you look, now and throughout our history, you find people espousing it as the key behavioral tenet.

It is the GOLDEN RULE

and it is perhaps the most simple, profound, and universal guide for human interaction.

Looking for a "crash course" on doing what's right? Here it is ...

> *Treat people the way you would like to be treated.*
>
> *Do unto others the way you would have them do unto you ... and the people you care about.*

When J. C. Penney opened his first dry goods store in Kemmerer, Wyoming, in 1902, he named it THE GOLDEN RULE. Why? Because **"Golden Rule principles are just as necessary for operating a business profitably as are trucks, typewriters, or twine,"** he said.

Leon Leonwood "L.L." Bean, was born in the small township of Greenwood, Maine, in 1872. The values he was raised to believe in were simple and deeply engrained. Nature was something to be revered. Family ties were a priority. And **"do unto others"** was not just a saying but a way of life. When Bean launched his company with the first Maine Hunting Shoe in 1912, he believed so strongly in the **GOLDEN RULE** that he made it the foundation of his business.

We have COMMITTED the Golden Rule to memory. Let us now commit it to life.

~ Edwin Markham ~

5

CHARACTER IS THE KEY.

COMMITMENT

Think of someone you know (or know of) who is **"a person of good character."** Lock his or her image in your mind. Now take a moment to reflect on the things this person says and does ... the personal characteristics that make him or her a role model for you. What comes to mind? What do you see?

Chances are that high on the list of your role model's qualities is **COMMITMENT** – the unwavering dedication to being a good family member and friend ... to doing his or her best at work and away from the job ... to doing what's right, noble, and decent.

Committed people like your role model just seem to have their heads and hearts in the right place. They keep their priorities straight. They stay focused on what's important. They know, inherently, that **what they believe must drive how they behave** – and how they behave ultimately determines the character they possess, the reputation they enjoy, and the legacy they leave.

Do they face occasional temptations to compromise their values ... to do what's easy, convenient, and self-serving? Of course they do! But they fight those temptations the same way they approach every aspect of their lives: **WITH EVERYTHING THEY HAVE.**

QUESTIONS TO PONDER

What am I committed to?

What values are important to me?

How committed am I?

What personal behaviors can I cite as evidence of those commitments?

How close are my behaviors to those of my commitment role model?

What can I do to be a commitment role model for others?

C
H
A
R
A
C
T
E
R

"COMMITMENT is what transforms
a promise into reality. It is the words that speak boldly of your intentions. And the actions which speak louder than the words.

It is making the time when there is none. Coming through time after time after time, year after year after year. Commitment is the stuff character is made of; the power to change the face of things. It is the daily triumph of integrity over skepticism."

~ ABRAHAM LINCOLN ~

One evening, after yet another of his magnificent concerts, world renowned pianist Van Cliburn was approached by an admirer who had been in the audience.

Obviously touched by the performance, the emotional fan grasped Cliburn's hand and said:

"I would give my life to be able to play the piano like that."

The pianist smiled and replied,

"I DID."

HONESTY

By its most basic definition, "honesty" means telling the truth ... avoiding deceptive or fraudulent behaviors ... refusing to lie, cheat, or steal. And when it comes to displaying good character, that age-old saying is generally as true now as it was when we first heard it as children:

HONESTY IS THE BEST POLICY!

Notice we used the word "generally." That's because, as we've become older (and hopefully wiser), we've discovered a couple of things about this subject:

1. Tactful honesty is good, but *brutal* honesty tends to be hurtful and counterproductive. With few exceptions, there's always a tactful way to get your message across. Find it and use it.

2. "Little white lies" are acceptable in those rare situations where being totally truthful would accomplish nothing more than making someone feel bad (e.g., *Do you like my present, Daddy?*).

A few words of caution about little white lies: They can easily become habitual, everyone's definition of "little" is different, and they still are lies.

TACTFUL HONESTY REALLY IS YOUR BEST POLICY!

Some time ago, there was an article about Ruben Gonzalez, who was playing in the final match of his very first professional racquetball tournament. He was competing against the long-reigning champion – seeking his first victory on the sport's pro circuit.

At match point in the final game, Gonzalez hammered a non-returnable "kill shot" into the front corner to win the event. The referee signaled that the shot was good, the linesman confirmed his call, and the crowd cheered the new winner. But after a brief hesitation, Gonzalez turned to the officials and declared that his shot actually had skipped into the wall, hitting the floor first. As a result, the match continued and the serve went to his opponent – who went on to win the tournament. Everyone was stunned as Gonzalez left the court.

The next issue of a popular racquetball magazine featured Ruben on its cover. In an interview article, the player was questioned about the occurrence. The interviewer probed Gonzalez. Here was a player with the outcome officially in his favor, with victory in his hands, who disqualifies himself at match point and then loses.

When asked why he did it, Gonzalez replied that he knew he had to be honest and tell the truth.

"IT WAS THE ONLY THING I COULD DO TO MAINTAIN MY INTEGRITY."

A plaque is displayed at the entrance to the
Vanderbilt University Student Center which reads:

TODAY I AM GOING TO GIVE YOU TWO EXAMINATIONS,

ONE IN TRIGONOMETRY AND ONE IN HONESTY.

I HOPE YOU WILL PASS THEM BOTH, BUT IF YOU

MUST FAIL ONE, LET IT BE TRIGONOMETRY.

The center is named for the author of that
statement, Madison Sarratt, and was installed
in 1993 by the Undergraduate Honor Council.

The best mind-altering drug is

TRUTH.

~ LILY TOMLIN ~

ACCOUNTABILITY

You know, one of the really nice things about our world is that it's full of people who have all kinds of good intentions – including the desire to consistently do what's right, fair, and just. But, intending or wanting to do something and actually doing it aren't the same. **THE DIFFERENCE IS ACTION.** And the thing that helps ensure action happens is **ACCOUNTABILITY.**

Remember when you were in your early teens? We do. We could hardly wait to become adults because we thought it would mean we could do whatever we wanted. Well, we became adults (at least age wise) and we found it meant something much different: Now WE were responsible for ourselves – WE were accountable for our actions. We still are ... and always will be.

Certainly, each of us has to answer to the external authorities in our lives like the government, our workplace leaders, and the "higher authority" that exists for many of us. But equally (if not more) important, we need to answer to ourselves. In the real world, others can mandate that we follow rules and laws, but they can't force us to be people of good character ... individuals who remain true to our beliefs and values. Ultimately, it's up to each of us to choose how we will live our lives, hold ourselves to high standards, and continually evaluate what's inside the image we see in the mirror.

"One of the annoying things about believing in free choice and individual responsibility is the difficulty of finding someone to blame your problems on.

And when you do find somebody, it's remarkable how often his picture turns up on your driver's license."

~ P. J. O'Rourke ~

THE FINAL FORMING OF A PERSON'S

CHARACTER

LIES IN THEIR OWN HANDS.

~ Anne Frank ~

A friend in the restaurant business was working the front register one evening when a family entered the establishment and approached him. As he was going through his standard customer welcoming spiel, the male adult of the group handed our friend three $100 bills — folded in half and bound together by a large paper clip. Jokingly, our friend told the man:

"SIR, THIS ISN'T VEGAS.
YOU DON'T HAVE TO TIP ME TO GET A GOOD TABLE."

The man replied, "Oh no, that's not a tip. I found it in the parking lot. It must belong to one of your customers or employees."

Impressed by the man's action, the restaurateur asked for his name and phone number — suggesting that if no one claimed the money, it would be returned to the finder. Then, as he seated the group, our friend leaned over to the man and said, "I have to ask you. That was a lot of money ... why did you turn it in?" Without hesitation, the man answered: "Because it doesn't belong to me."

"Well you definitely are an honest man," our friend replied, "especially since no one would have known if you had just kept it." "Well that's not exactly true," the man said as he pointed to his family. "They would have known. More importantly ...

I WOULD HAVE KNOWN."

RESPECT

Everyone wants it, everyone needs it. It's a critical building block of good character ... and it's something that most of us could stand to ratchet up a little.

It is RESPECT.

As we see it, there are two types of respect. First is basic human respect — the kind you're entitled to merely by being born. Everyone deserves it equally because through birth, everyone is equal — we're all living, breathing human beings. This first type of respect is based on the fact that other people's needs, hopes, rights, dreams, ideas, and inherent worth are just as important and valuable as our own. And it's demonstrated by treating others with dignity and courtesy.

The second type of respect is one that we **EARN** by our actions. This is different from the first type because **it's based on who we are** (the quality of our characters) rather than what we are (human beings); it comes from behavior rather than mere birth. Accordingly, if we want our judgment, opinions, and skills respected, we have to earn that by demonstrating judgment, opinions, and skills that are **respectABLE**. If we want to be respected for dependability, we must earn that respect by consistently BEING dependable. And, if we wish to be respected as values-driven people, we must earn that respect as well – **by continually "walking our talk."**

> **"Be beautiful if you can, wise if you want to.**
>
> **But be respected ... that is essential."**
>
> ~ ANNA GOULD ~

C
H
A
R
A
C
T
E
R

RESPECT

▶ **R**ECOGNIZE the inherent worth of all human beings.

▶ **E**LIMINATE derogatory words and phrases from your vocabulary.

▶ **S**PEAK *with* people – not *at* them ... or *about* them.

▶ **P**RACTICE empathy. Walk awhile in others' shoes.

▶ **E**ARN respect from others through respect-worthy behaviors.

▶ **C**ONSIDER others' feelings before speaking and acting.

▶ **T**REAT everyone with dignity and courtesy.

I'm not concerned with your liking or disliking me ... all I ask is that you

RESPECT ME AS A HUMAN BEING.

~ JACKIE ROBINSON ~

ATTITUDE

Over the years, we've discovered that one of the many commonalties among people of good character is that each has "an attitude." More accurately, each has *three* attitudes – all of which are factors that lead to personal success.

THE FIRST OF THESE ATTITUDES TAKES THE FORM OF A CONTAGIOUS, UPBEAT OUTLOOK. People who exhibit this are generally positive, approachable, and cooperative. For them, the glass is almost always "half full." Do they ever get down and have bad days? Sure ... they're human! But they typically bounce back quickly – choosing to be **victors** rather than **victims**.

THE SECOND ATTITUDE IS A CAN-DO SPIRIT. Here, the mentality is: *Give me a task and I'm all over it! We can do this. Let's get to it.* People with this mindset focus on making things work rather than on lamenting on why they won't. That's why these folks are the DOERS of the world.

FINALLY, INDIVIDUALS OF GOOD CHARACTER DISPLAY WHAT WE CALL AN "ATTITUDE OF GRATITUDE." They appreciate the people they know, the things they have, and the opportunities they're afforded ... and they SHOW it!

Looking to make your character even stronger?

Get some attitude!

C H A R A C T E R

There is little difference in people,
but that little difference makes a
big difference.

That little difference is **attitude**.
The big difference is whether
it is positive or negative.

~ W. CLEMENT STONE ~

COURAGE

QUESTION: What does "courage" have to do with being a person of good character ... with someone who stays true to honorable principles and noble values?

ANSWER: EVERYTHING!

You see, being values-driven means two things:

1. **Doing what's right** — following our conscience; refusing to compromise ourselves, or our principles, despite pressures and temptations to the contrary, and

2. **Taking a stand against what's wrong** — speaking out, and acting out, whenever we see others do things that are incorrect or inappropriate.

Unquestionably, both of those require guts, nerve, and fortitude ... they require courage. And individuals who do them consistently are truly courageous people. With that as a given, each of us needs to think about, and answer for ourselves, one simple question:

HOW COURAGEOUS AM I?

Courage is ...

Following your conscience instead of "following the crowd."

Refusing to take part in hurtful or disrespectful behaviors.

Sacrificing personal gain for the benefit of others.

Speaking your mind even though others don't agree.

Taking complete responsibility for your actions ...
and your mistakes.

Following the rules – and insisting that others do the same.

Challenging the status quo in search of better ways.

Doing what you know is right – regardless of the risks
and potential consequences.

C
H
A
R
A
C
T
E
R

Make us to choose the harder right instead of the easier wrong, and never to be content with a half truth when the whole truth can be won. Endow us with courage that is born of loyalty to all that is noble and worthy, that scorns to compromise with vice and injustice and knows no fear when truth and right are in jeopardy.

"CADET PRAYER"

repeated during chapel services at the U.S. Military Academy.

TRUST

HAVE YOU EVER KNOWN A PERSON OF GOOD CHARACTER WHOM YOU DIDN'T TRUST?

Of course not! Character and trust – or more accurately, trustworthiness – go hand in hand. **Good people just naturally do things that EARN them the trust of others.** They are honest and open ... competent and knowledgeable. They are consistent and considerate. They display concern for others' well being as well as their own – sometimes *before* their own. And most importantly, they honor their promises and commitments.

For trustworthy people, their word is their bond. If they say they'll do something – whether "important" or seemingly insignificant – they make sure they remember it ... and they DO it. They count on the fact that others can count on *them*. And they understand that statements like "I was gonna," "I meant to," and "I haven't forgotten" all translate the same way: **I JUST DIDN'T DO IT!** Those are excuses; they're rationalizations for inaction. And as such, they're close to meaningless.

As we've said before, most individuals really are well meaning. With few exceptions, all people intend to keep their word. But good intentions alone won't carry the day. Fact is, we get no "points" for them. Points come only when we deliver ... when we DO things that are trustworthy ... when we walk our talk.

> **NO, I DON'T UNDERSTAND**
> **MY HUSBAND'S THEORY OF RELATIVITY.**
> **BUT I KNOW MY HUSBAND,**
> **AND I KNOW HE CAN BE TRUSTED.**
>
> ~ ELSA EINSTEIN ~

DO YOU?

Trustworthy people keep their promises and commitments. If they say they'll do something, they remember it – and they DO IT! **DO YOU?**

Trustworthy people operate "in the open." They avoid hidden agendas and going behind people's backs when pursuing their goals. **DO YOU?**

Trustworthy people admit to their mistakes – and correct them. They avoid blaming others for their errors and failures. **DO YOU?**

Trustworthy people don't take what isn't theirs and refuse to accept what they haven't rightfully earned. **DO YOU?**

Trustworthy people honor confidentiality. They maintain the security of sensitive information that is appropriately restricted to certain eyes and ears only. **DO YOU?**

Trustworthy people carry their share of the load. They do their jobs and meet their assigned responsibilities without the need for continual monitoring or prodding. **DO YOU?**

ETHICS & INTEGRITY

You read about them in the papers; you hear about them on the evening news; they are plastered on industry publications and legal journals. People constantly talk about them, and almost everywhere you turn they continue to be front page news. They are "ethics" and "integrity." **And together they not only are the essence of good character but also one of society's most pressing concerns.**

Fortunately, the ethics and integrity lapses that make all the headlines are behavioral exceptions rather than the rule. Fact is, most people do mostly right things most of the time. And that's truly encouraging and uplifting. But it's in the difference between **"most"** and **"all"** (most people vs. all people; mostly right things vs. always right things; most of the time vs. all of the time) where the challenge of doing right is found – and where the greatest opportunity for ethical enhancement exists.

To be sure, none of us is perfect. And that needs to be seen for exactly what it is: **A FACT ... A CONDITION, NOT AN EXCUSE.** Compensating for our imperfections and overcoming the temptations we face require commitment and self-discipline. Behaving ethically – **being people of integrity – isn't always easy, but it is always RIGHT!** It is a requirement for long-term success, and it is what "walking the talk" is all about.

REAL **INTEGRITY** IS DOING
THE **RIGHT THING**, KNOWING THAT
NOBODY'S GOING TO KNOW
WHETHER YOU DID IT OR NOT.

~ OPRAH WINFREY ~

C
H
A
R
A
C
T
E
R

THINKING YOUR WAY TO ETHICS

A while back, we spent considerable time collecting background data for two handbooks we would later publish entitled *Ethics4Everyone* and *Leading to Ethics.* As part of our research, we read volumes of information, and studied scores of individuals, to "get a handle" on our topic. Here's what we concluded:

While "ethics" is an extensive and somewhat complex subject, the number one (and probably most important) key to consistently doing what's right is actually quite simple – **think before you act**. Behaviorally, that means testing decisions and planned activities for "rightness" before implementing them.

And here's the test:

1. **Is it legal?**
2. **Is it in sync with my values?**
3. **Will I be comfortable and guilt-free if I do it?**
4. **Would I do it to my family and friends?**
5. **Would I be perfectly okay with someone doing it to me?**
6. **Would the most ethical person I know do it?**

When decorated war hero and baseball great Ted Williams turned 40 and was approaching the end of his career, he slipped into a batting slump — hitting less than .300... At the time, he was the highest-paid player in the game —

EARNING $125,000 PER YEAR.

But when the Red Sox offered to renew his contract for the same amount, he objected. Was he looking for more money? ABSOLUTELY NOT!

To the contrary, he announced that he had not earned the then generous salary his team was willing to pay. Believing he had failed to give the team and fans their money's worth, he cut his own salary by twenty- five percent!

RESPONSIBILITY

Ever wonder who **THEY** are?

THEY seem to be everywhere. **THEY** must be a big and powerful group with a great deal of influence, because we sure do talk about them a lot:

"They should know better!"

"That's their problem!"

"They need to do something about this!"

"It's all because of them!"

"They're the ones who fouled things up!"

No need to ask if those sound familiar. Who among us hasn't pointed a finger at **THEM** before?

"They" and "them" are common pronouns – part of normal, everyday speech. We utter them all the time. And when it comes to building good character and walking the talk, they may be the absolute *worst* words in our language. Why? Just look at what "they" and "them" mean: OTHER PEOPLE, SOMEONE ELSE. You don't have to be a genius to know that those words are dripping with non-responsibility.

Maybe it's time we all did some word switching.

Imagine what would happen – think of how our perspectives might change – if we stopped using "they," "them," and "their" altogether, and instead used "we," "us," and "our."

Let's see:

"~~THEY~~ WE NEED TO DO SOMETHING ABOUT THIS!"

"THAT'S ~~THEIR~~ OUR PROBLEM!"

"IT'S UP TO ~~THEM~~ US!"

"~~THEY~~ WE NEED TO DO WHAT'S RIGHT.

See and feel the difference?

So, the next time you catch yourself starting to say or think the T-word ("they"), use "we" instead. After all, the first step in meeting our responsibilities as adults is acknowledging that we have them.

You know, pointing the finger at **them** probably is a waste of time, anyway. We're beginning to think **they** don't exist. Because ...

**Every time we've gone looking for "them,"
all we've found is US!**

GETTING IN SHAPE

Looking to build or strengthen your Character muscles? Here are some exercises ... TO AVOID:

- ► **JUMPING** to conclusions
- ► **PASSING** the buck
- ► **GRABBING** the credit
- ► **THROWING** your weight around
- ► **STRETCHING** the truth
- ► **BENDING** the rules
- ► **BREAKING** your promises
- ► **PULLING** a fast one
- ► **STEPPING** on others
- ► **DODGING** your duty
- ► **RUNNING** your mouth off
- ► **"LIFTING"** what isn't yours

We have the BILL OF RIGHTS.
What we need is a
BILL OF RESPONSIBILITIES.

~ BILL MAHER ~

I think we all have a
little voice inside us
that will guide us ...
if we shut out all the
noise and clutter from
our lives and listen
to that voice, it will
tell us the right
thing to do.

~ CHRISTOPHER REEVE ~

Choices

OUR CHARACTERS SHOW IN ...

The jokes we **CHOOSE** to share ... and not to share.

The derogatory terms we **CHOOSE** to use ... and refuse to use.

The promises we **CHOOSE** to break ... and the ones we keep.

The rumors we **CHOOSE** to spread ... and those we ignore.

The resources we **CHOOSE** to waste ... and those we use wisely.

The lies we **CHOOSE** to tell ... and not to tell.

The responsibilities we **CHOOSE** to accept ... and those we shirk.

The courtesies we **CHOOSE** to extend ... and fail to extend.

The efforts we **CHOOSE** to put forth ... and not put forth.

The quality we **CHOOSE** to provide ... and the corners we cut.

The information we **CHOOSE** to share ... and that which we hoard.

The listening we **CHOOSE** to do ... and not do.

The respect we **CHOOSE** to give ... and fail to give.

The helpful hands we **CHOOSE** to extend ...
                                   and those we keep in our pockets.

A POEM of **POSSIBILITIES**

If every person walked the talk,
can you imagine
how it would be?

A world filled with good intentions ..

. . . that all became reality.

We could count on one another,
and coexist respectfully.
There would be no
broken promises,

and no hypocrisy.

*We'd have no problem spotting heroes,
they'd be everywhere to see.*

*Just by looking in the mirror,
we all would find …*

INTEGRITY.

If everybody did what's right, most rules we wouldn't need.

Conscience, trust,
and common sense

would be the things
that we'd all heed.

There would be no hurtful
actions in the news
that we would read.

Only story, after story,
of yet another

noble deed.

And when it came to raising
children with young characters
to mold and feed,
the best lessons
they could ever learn
would come by merely following ...

OUR lead.

If each of us behaved beliefs,
there'd be little cause for fear.

All actions would be honorable,
our values would be clear.

*Just by watching
what it is we DO,*

*one could tell
what we hold dear.
For our principles would be
acts you see ...*

*Not merely words
you hear.*

It's a challenging task to
Walk the Talk ...

every hour, day, and year.

And we ALL can do a better job,
*   let's start RIGHT NOW …*

...RIGHT HERE!

CLOSING THOUGHTS

Life is an ongoing process with many beginnings and continuations, and lots of possibilities.

There's no point at which we've learned everything we ever need to know, become as healthy as we ever need to be, or done every good thing we could possibly do. There's also no point at which we've lived as true to our values as we ever need to live. That's why walking the talk, like life itself, is a journey rather than a destination.

There's always another road to travel, another new path to take. The goal is not to "get there" but instead to make sure you keep moving in the right direction. And to do that, you need a combination of faith and conviction.

You need to ...

BELIEVE THAT WALKING THE TALK MATTERS

and, most importantly, you need to ...

BELIEVE THAT YOU CAN MAKE A DIFFERENCE.

BELIEVE THAT IT MATTERS

As each of us grapples with the challenge of keeping our behaviors in sync with good and important values, we may occasionally be tempted to ask ourselves a simple yet profound question:

Why bother to walk the talk?

In response to that question, we offer the following:

Because it defines who we are – and how we are judged.

Without question, the degree to which we are values-driven defines the people we are, the reputations we enjoy, and the legacies we leave. It determines how we are seen now, and how we will be remembered later.

As humans, we tend to judge ourselves by our intentions, but others judge us by our behaviors and actions. And how we are perceived and judged by others has a lot to do with the success we ultimately enjoy.

Because it benefits others.

When we walk the talk, we influence and positively impact the people we touch, interact with, and care about. They benefit when we are respectful. They benefit when we take responsibility for doing right and carrying our share of the load. And they benefit when we set the example for ethics and integrity.

Because our children are watching.

They're watching ... and learning. And they rightfully assume that our behaviors are the standards that they should follow. We must show them the way ... we cannot let them down.

Don't worry that children never listen to you;
worry that they are always watching you.   ~ Robert Fulghum ~

Because it's simply the right thing to do.

A naive statement? We don't think so. Idealistic? Guilty as charged. But the way we see it, if we truly are good people, then no other reason is better ... no other reason is necessary.

Most importantly ...

Believe that YOU can make a difference.

It's an age-old question: Can one person REALLY make a difference? Well, we only need to dust off our history books to find plenty of evidence that one person CAN. From Thomas Jefferson, Abraham Lincoln, and Martin Luther King, Jr. – to Mother Teresa, Rosa Parks, and Marie Curie – history is loaded with positive proof of the impact individuals can have. Granted, these are a few of the big names, but there are plenty of less famous folks who have left (and are leaving) their footprints on their world, their workplaces, and their communities – day in and day out.

One of them was a little girl named Alex.

Back in 2000, a young cancer patient was driven to do something very right ... to walk her talk when it came to caring for others. Her name was Alexandra ("Alex") Scott, and she came up with a rather simple idea: She would set up a lemonade stand and raise money to help find a cure for kids with cancer. So, with the help of her older brother, she assembled "Alex's Lemonade Stand for Childhood Cancer" on the front lawn of her home.

Although her health was deteriorating and her condition worsening, Alex continued to hold an annual lemonade sale for the next four years — with all of her "profits" going to childhood cancer research.

As a result of the inspirational example of this tiny young girl with a weak body but enormous heart, literally thousands of lemonade stands and other fundraising events have been held across the country. Sponsored by children, schools, businesses, and service organizations, they benefit the Alex's Lemonade Stand Foundation for childhood cancer established by her family and many friends. As of 2007, the foundation has raised over $12 million for childhood cancer research.

On August 1st, 2004, "Alex" Scott died peacefully at the age of eight. While she will greatly be missed by all who knew her and knew of her, Alex's short yet unforgettable life truly is a celebration of the human spirit.

So, the next time you wonder if one person can make a difference, think of Alex — one little girl who literally took lemons and made lemonade ... one little soul who inspires all of us to walk our talk.

Note: For information on the Alex's Lemonade Stand Foundation, please visit alexslemonade.org.

FINALLY...

Start each new day with a commitment to do what's right – regardless of what may come your way.

If you slip and make a mistake, fix it, learn from it, and move on. There's no time to sulk or dwell on the past. **LIFE IS TOO SHORT.**

If you get knocked down, push yourself back up again. Fight harder to stay on your feet ... and to avoid despair. **LIFE COMES WITH STRUGGLES.**

If you're doing everything right but can't seem to come out on top, be patient. Hold the course. Success is rarely an immediate, overnight thing. **LIFE FREQUENTLY MAKES US WAIT.**

When you do succeed, take the time to enjoy it. Savor it. Take pride in yourself. Appreciate your accomplishments ... and the people who helped you make them. **LIFE OFFERS MANY JOYS.**

Remember that with each sunrise comes new opportunities. Yesterday is history. Today offers a clean slate upon which to record your life ... and your legacy.

When you wake up, seek the courage and strength to do the right thing. Decide that this will be another day in which you ...

WALK THE TALK.

ERIC HARVEY, president and founder of The WALK THE TALK®
Company – WalkTheTalk.com – is a leading expert on Ethics and
Values-Based Practices. He is a renowned business consultant
and the author of twenty-eight highly-acclaimed books – including the
best-selling ***Walk The Talk... And Get The Results You Want***,
Ethics4Everyone, and ***The Leadership Secrets of Santa Claus***.
He and his team of professionals have helped thousands of individuals
and organizations turn their values into value-added results.

STEVE VENTURA is a recognized and respected author,
book producer, and award-winning training program designer.
His work reflects over 30 years of human resource development
experience – both as a practitioner and a business consultant.
His prior books include **Start Right ... Stay Right**, **Walk Awhile
In My Shoes**, **Five Star Teamwork**, **What to Do When Conflict Happens**,
and **Yes Lives in the Land of No. Walk The Talk** is the fourth work
he has co-authored with Eric Harvey.

WALK *the* **TALK** is offered to you by

The WALK THE TALK® Company

If you have enjoyed this high-impact resource and would like
to order additional copies, please contact one of our Customer
Satisfaction Representatives at

1.888.822.9255
or order online at
www.WalkTheTalk.com

While you are visiting our website, be sure to check out
our online bookstore to learn more about our complete
library of employee, leadership, and organizational
development resources.

WALKTHETALK.COM

Resources for Personal and Professional Success